THE BIBLE AND DECISION MAKING

The Bible and Decision Making

inSIGHTS

BIBLE STUDIES FOR GROWING
F A I T H

Stephanie Boughton Haines

WIPF & STOCK · Eugene, Oregon

Wipf and Stock Publishers
199 W 8th Ave, Suite 3
Eugene, OR 97401

The Bible and Decision Making
By Haines, Stephanie Boughton
Copyright©2001 Pilgrim Press
ISBN 13: 978-1-60899-224-9
Publication date 1/15/2010
Previously published by Pilgrim Press, 2001

Contents

User's Guide

Bible study can be one of life's most exciting adventures. It can deepen faith, spark action, cause change, rekindle commitment, force an issue, and transform lives. It can also confound settled ideas; confuse certainty; question faith; trouble complacency; and unsettle tidy, organized, and compartmentalized lives. Bible study can "bring down the powerful from their thrones, and lift up the lowly; it can fill the hungry with good things, and send the rich away empty" (Luke 2:52–53). How can Bible study create such a stir? Because it can be an encounter, an epiphany, a mountaintop experience, a radically life-changing meeting with "I am what I am; I am what I will be; I am what the future will need."

Bible study is a task and a privilege. We members of mainline denominations often feel confused and unsettled when confronted by our more fundamentalist brothers and sisters who have spent many hours in serious Bible study. They seem able to quote and proof text no matter what the situation. I do not suggest that we adopt the same tactics. I do suggest that we take seriously the requirement to know and understand the scriptures so that we become biblically knowledgeable and theologically savvy. We have a responsibility as Christians to know the Bible, to study regularly, to think deeply, to engage with others in the struggle to understand and interpret the faith for our own generations. Ours is a living faith in a living God that demands we encounter for ourselves the stories that have shaped the great cloud of witnesses who preceded us in the journey that is our faith.

The Bible and Decision Making is a six-week adult Bible study that can be used in a variety of settings:

- Sunday morning adult class

- new members' class

- Advent or Lent seasonal study group

- faith formation class

Encourage attendees to bring their own Bibles, but also have a number of different translations on hand for comparison and amplification.

Arrange the room so that people can see each other easily. No one should face someone else's back. I also suggest a focus point in the center of the group — a cloth on which you place a lit candle. Then add one or more additional items — a flower in a vase, an interesting rock or other found object, a bowl of fruit (to be shared at break time), a small sculpture.

Study questions follow each section. Have newsprint and markers for recording answers to questions and noting additional questions participants may have.

Practical Suggestions for Bible Study

One of the wonderful things about the Bible, with all its stories, is that it allows us, within certain limits, to be interpreters. It is open to you and me as we bring our own experiences to it. Bible study does not need to be boring, nor should it be. In the words of Martin Luther, "God's word has hands and feet. It runs after you. It grips you. Let it loose, then things will happen." The following suggestions might be helpful to your group:

1. Read the text from several different translations, versions, or paraphrases. Note the differences in the readings. Have several persons read the passage aloud.

2. Center yourself on the text. Get into the text by asking:

   (a) What questions, images, thoughts, or feelings does this passage evoke for me?

   (b) With what character do I identify in this passage? What is it that a particular character is saying to me?

   (c) What is the passage really saying? Don't be concerned with "did this really happen?" Rather, look more closely at what the passage means.

3. Get into the Scriptures by role playing or creating a drama about the passage — actually be the characters. You will discover that many of the passages can be written as plays, with or without narration. Be creative. It is not sacrilegious to explore ways to interpret the meanings of texts for us in this day and age or extract personal meaning on our own religious and spiritual journeys. Let the Bible speak to you. Do not confine your thinking to how it has always been. Contemporize the event, characters, and message as much as possible. What does it mean or what could it mean for you today?

4. Use your imagination. Many Scripture passages can be interpreted in several different ways. Try to understand the themes, and then "plug" them into your life and your faith experience, Examples: God's fairness, Jesus' inclusiveness and concern for the outcast, the lonely, the fearful.

Introduction

Have a decision to make? Hold a Bible upside down by its spine, while closing your eyes very tightly. No peeking now. Ask the question for which you need an answer — any question. Should I change jobs or stay where I am? My kid really needs the discipline of martial arts training, but I don't know if I can afford it. What should I do? I'm going gray far too quickly, should I dye my hair or leave it the way it is? Flip the Bible over, allowing it to open. With eyes still clenched tightly shut, place your index finger anywhere on the open pages. Open your eyes and read. There is your answer; your decision is made — the Bible and decision making.

We Christians want to use the knowledge and insight of scripture to help us in our daily lives. The process mentioned above is but one variety among many for blindly using the Bible for help in getting through ordinary, daily life. I do not recommend it. That question about the gray hair is mine. I held the Bible by its spine, closed my eyes tightly, flipped it over, used my index finger to locate a spot on the page, opened my eyes and read: "Whoever winks the eye causes trouble, but the one who rebukes boldly makes peace" (Proverbs 10:10). What does that mean? What does it mean about my gray hair? Should I or shouldn't I?

Every day we make thousands of decisions: what time to set the alarm clock, what to wear to work, who to talk with on the phone, how fast to drive, whether to eat a salad or a burrito for lunch, how to ask for additional time off, where to take the kids for some quality time together, whether to argue with someone or let the incident pass, what television programs to watch, what book to read, who to thank. The vast majority of our decisions seem to take little or no deep thought. They cause us brief or no anxiety, confront us with few dilemmas, and challenge us hardly at all.

And then, just when we are comfortable and skipping merrily along, we are forced to make difficult decisions, decisions that could change the direction of our lives, decisions that could have consequences for the people we love, decisions that seem so difficult that we do not know where to begin or how to proceed. A spouse is afflicted with cancer and the medical establishment says nothing else can be done. What do you do? Your boss informs you that your job is being transferred, and you must relocate or lose your position. Your family does not want to move. What do you do? Your youngest child is experiencing discrimination in high school because she has announced she is a lesbian. You think she's going through a phase and do not know anything about homosexuality anyway. What do you do? Sometimes we cannot even see that we have options. Sometimes we are overwhelmed and paralyzed, stricken powerless by circumstances. Sometimes, even more basic, we do not know who we are. How can we know what to do?

There is no substitute for direct, divine revelation. Unfortunately most of us are not going to encounter a burning bush, or experience a vision, or meet God face to face. We can, however, rely on scripture to direct us through the murky mists of daily human life. The random meeting with a particular text, as mentioned in the first paragraph will not ably assist. But careful, regular study of scripture will give us a foundation, a base from which to begin, a life raft in turbulent water, a peek into the mind of God so that when decision time comes, as it always does, we will know who we are and how others who encountered God responded in similar situations.

May you go with God on this great adventure.

Sessions One and Two focus on our identity as persons of faith. Sessions Three and Four examine how some biblical characters respond to encounter with life-changing situations. Sessions Five and Six deal with direct admonitions for human behavior.

STEPHANIE BOUGHTON HAINES

Genesis 1:24–31

THE SIXTH DAY

◈

Notes to the leader:

Although Session One will focus on Genesis 1:24–31, setting the creation of humankind in context might be helpful. The Creation Story, Genesis 1:1–2:3, easily lends itself to an antiphonal reading or telling. One person tells the story of each day's happenings and ends the telling with these words: "And God looked at all that had been created and said." The rest of the group responds in unison: "That's good!" The leader finishes: "And there was evening and there was morning, the _____ day." On the seventh day, there will be no response.

Arrange the room or tables so that folks are sitting in a circle. No one should be facing into someone else's back. Encourage people to bring their own Bibles for subsequent sessions. Have available a variety of translations for comparison and amplification, and for those who "just forgot" their own.

By the end of the fifth day, God had created most of what we know as creation. On the first day, God created a *dome*, which we know as the sky. People of the ancient world believed the sky to be solid, able to separate the upper realm from the lower waters. On the second day, the *seas* were in place, remnant of the watery chaos that existed before creation began, and were limited by the edges of Earth. On the third day God created only indirectly.

Mother Earth is commanded to become fertile, and "the earth brought forth *vegetation* of every kind." On the fourth day, God puts lights in the sky: the sun to brighten the day and the moon to lighten the night, and stars. These lights are just that, *lights*; they do not control human destiny as other ancient peoples believed. Therefore they were not to be worshipped. And the fifth day marks the first life on Earth, *fishes and birds.* God commands the waters to "bring forth swarms of living creatures and let the birds fly above earth." Everything that swims and everything that flies is encouraged to reproduce and occupy the whole of Earth. At the end of each day, God looked at what had been created and said, "That's good!"

On the sixth day, God creates all the *creatures that inhabit the dry land.* Mother Earth is again the mediator of the creation of all the land animals, "living creatures of every kind: cattle and creeping things and wild animals of the earth of every kind." Finally, on the last half of the sixth day, God creates *human beings.* But God does not create alone! God says, "Let us make humankind in our image, according to our likeness." God seems to be consulting other divine beings, those who are not God, although we do not know who they are. These entities are called and consulted and participate in the creation of humankind. Think about the idea that God is not in heaven alone; others are there, others who are worthy of being a part of the central act of creation! When God creates people, God chooses to share the creation! Here in the very first chapter of the very first book of the Bible, God is in relationship. God is not some cosmic Lone Ranger setting the world in place and at right all alone; God invites the participation of others.

The text says that humans are created in the "image of God." Scholars have been discussing what this phrase means for centuries. Although no one can determine in absolute fact, it appears to imply that people are more than they seem. A dog is a dog. A cow is a cow. A bird is a bird. But human beings are not just human beings; they are fashioned from a blueprint that includes attributes of the divine. Part of that blueprint is the ability to have communication between humans and God, God and humans. Although not stated, we can assume that other creatures do not communicate with God, at least not in the same way we are capable. In addition, humanity is given the gifts that will permit them to pursue their God-given responsibilities.

In the ancient world, the ruler — the king — alone was construed to be created in the image of God. The king, therefore, was ruling on God's behalf, purportedly doing what God wanted, and therefore above questioning. Here in Genesis, we find that not only kings, but all humanity is created in the image of God. "Male and female [God] created them" which means that the female is as much in the image of God as is the male. To concentrate solely on male images and male attributes of God is to miss a considerable wealth of information we can discover about God by including female attributes and images in our quest to understand the nature of God. That both female and male are mentioned in the creation story implies that what they will do in life will not be identical. These verses can also be used to substantiate the claim that God can and should be identified by female images as well as male — mother as well as father, she as well as he.

God addresses both the male and the female in v. 28 with the command to "be fruitful and multiply, and fill the earth and subdue it; and have dominion over the fish of the sea and over the birds of the air and over every living thing that moves upon the earth." This one little verse has been used perhaps not always blatantly, but subtlety, to justify doing whatever we human beings wanted to do to Earth and the other living creatures that share this sphere with us. In fact, the text has no implication even remotely designating that kind of license. God has given humanity responsibility to exercise creative power. We can reproduce ourselves as can all the other creatures. And we are given the privilege and honor to care for Earth and its creatures, nurturing and loving what God has called into being. We are to help, to facilitate the world to reach its greatest potential.

Finally, God describes what I call the "vegetarian imperative." Human dominion is not to involve killing. People are to eat of the seeds and plants that God has provided and are not given permission to kill other creatures for food. I am reminded of a bumper sticker I see regularly as I drive my dogs to the park for their afternoon walk: MEAT IS MURDER. According to the creation story, this little statement is true and we slaughter our way through history at our own peril.

On the seventh day God rests because of all the work that had been done.

Questions for Reflection and Discussion

To the leader:

> *In order for the members of your Bible study group to deepen their relationships with other members and feel relatively safe at the same time, I recommend that you use a variety of configurations for group discussion — diads, triads, or my favorite — the M&M scramble. Ahead of time, for example, if you have twenty folks in your group, separate out four red M&Ms, four green M&Ms, four yellow M&Ms, four orange M&Ms, and four blue M&Ms. Put the twenty M&Ms in a bowl and mix well. Holding the bowl so the participants cannot see into it, have each person pick one M&M. Then separate the group according to colors. Be sure to have the remainder of the bag available for consumption as one*

dinky dot of chocolate will hardly be enough for most folks. Some large group discussion is also valuable and useful, particularly on the most general questions.

When you work in small groups like those mentioned, it is often helpful to "report out" after discussion. Use newsprint and markers to record pertinent information that you or others might like to remember. Tape each completed sheet of newsprint to the wall so that you have a running history of your Bible study.

- How relevant do you consider the Genesis 1 story of creation to be to our modern world?

- How aware are you of the created world on a day to day basis?

- How much credence should school boards give the Genesis account of creation in science textbooks? How did you arrive at your answer?

- List all the attributes of God that you can think of; you need not confine yourself to this particular text. As you think of yourself made in the image of God, what qualities do you share with God?

- What does it mean to be created in the image of God? How do the words "created in the image of God" affect your relationships with other people?

- What does it mean to "have dominion over" and to "subdue" Earth?

- God has clearly appointed human beings to be stewards of all that was created. How does that stewardship influence your attitude toward and decisions about the environment? the other creatures that share Earth with us? your daily living in our consumer oriented culture?

- What is your reaction to the statement that v. 27 can be used to justify using female images for God? What are some of the female images for God already found in the Bible?

- How do you feel about the decision to use inclusive language in worship? Where do you stand and what is your rationale?

- If males and females have been created in the image of God and given equal responsibility to care for Earth and all creation, what are you doing to rectify women being assigned second class place?

- How do you understand the differences in males and females? According to the text, is one gender more important than the other?

- How does the creation story inform your behavior toward the rest of creation — water, air, sky, plants, and critters of land, air, and sea?

- What's your reaction to the "vegetarian imperative"? Have you ever thought of meat as murder? What will you prepare or order for supper tomorrow night?

- Write a paragraph about yourself, created in the image of God. Remember that you are so pleasing to God that God looked at you and said, "That's good!" How does being created in God's image influence your decision making?

Closing

Invite folks to stand in a circle holding hands. As the leader you say, "I'm going to start. I'll say my name and then tell you that I am made in the image of God and that God looked at me and said, 'That's good.' You will respond to me, saying back to me what I have just said to you." We'll go around the circle each person doing the same. We will all respond to each person.

Leader: My name is Stephanie. I am made in the image of God. God looked at me and said, "That's good."

All: Your name is Stephanie. You are made in the image of God. God looked at you and said, "That's good."

Proceed around the whole group. Leader, end with these words after all have spoken and been responded to: "Thanks be to God for all creation and for each and every one of us."

I Samuel 3:1–4:1a

SPEAK. I AM LISTENING

Notes to the leader:

This text lends itself to a dramatic reading using one person to be the narrator, one person to be Samuel, one person to be Eli, and one person to be God. The narrator reads all the material that is not spoken by the three characters. For this kind of reading, all participants should be using the same translation.

Arrange the room so that everyone can see everyone else. Seeing facial expressions and other's eyes help greatly to develop a community feeling and level of safety for the sharing of ideas and responses.

Samuel, a youth of about twelve years old, ministered to the Lord under the guidance of Eli. Eli was a priest who was very old and going blind. Eli cared for the Ark of the Lord in the temple which would have been, in this time before the Jerusalem Temple, a tent. As Dickens said in the beginning of *Great Expectations*, "These were the best of times. These were the worst of times." These times in which Samuel ministered were times of despair because Eli's sons were corrupt and their leadership suspect. The word of the Lord was rare and visions nearly non-existent. The Philistines were about to attack, threatening Israel's survival, and the need for a king to give strong, decisive leadership was pressing ever more heavily. Times were bad. Into this mix of general hopelessness comes the story of

Samuel's call and the possibility of new beginnings.

Samuel was asleep in the temple, close to the Ark of the Lord, while Eli slept some distance away in his own room. It was just before dawn, "the lamp of God [having] not yet gone out." God called, "Samuel, Samuel." Samuel responds, "Here I am," and runs to Eli and says, "Here I am, for you called me." But Eli had not called Samuel, "I did not call; lie down again." Two more times God calls, and Samuel runs to Eli.

Samuel did not yet know God personally. We can assume that Samuel knew about God because he had been working with and for Eli for a number of years. But he had not seen God face-to-face nor had any direct communication from God. We can also assume that while Samuel had been with Eli, God had rarely if ever communicated directly with Eli either. The third time that Samuel runs to Eli — Eli who is blind — "sees" that the voice Samuel hears belongs to God. He tells the youth that should he hear the voice again, he should respond, "Speak, Lord, for your servant is listening."

The fourth time, God not only calls but stands there calling, "Samuel! Samuel!" And Samuel responds, "Speak, for your servant is listening." God has some good news and some bad news. The bad news comes first. God is going to do something in Israel that will make the ears tingle of anyone who hears about it. God is going to punish Eli's house, his offspring, for the blaspheming they have done. Poor Eli was not able to keep them from it; even though he tried, they would not listen to him. Not only that, but Eli and his sons will not be able to expiate the curse with sacrifice or offerings ever. The good news is that the voice of the Lord is no longer silent, but will be heard through the voice of Samuel. It is important to note here that Samuel must discern God's word and pass it on to Israel, but Samuel's word will never be exactly the same as God's word. Any of us who preach would be wise to approach the task with humility as we struggle to discern what God is saying and then pass on the message in our own words, with our own understanding.

The vision and the voice disappear and Samuel lies there until morning comes, unable to sleep, knowing that Eli will probably ask for a report and fearing to tell what God has spoken. At dawn, Samuel opens the doors of the temple, and just as he is doing so, Eli calls to him, demanding a full report, telling him to hold nothing back. So Samuel relates all that the Lord has said, keeping nothing from Eli.

Samuel grows up, and God continues to speak with him, "let[ting] none of his words fall to the ground." All of Israel now knows that Samuel is an honest and sincere prophet of God. Oddly, God continues to appear to Samuel at Shiloh, the very place where the sons of Eli blasphemed and Eli heard no word from nor saw the Lord.

Many a preacher has used this text to illustrate a simple call story. However, it is unlike other call stories in a couple of distinct ways: it does not follow the classic call story where the person hears the call but expresses unworthiness to receive it, nor is there a commissioning for a specific prophetic purpose. Samuel's call is very unlike many a religious mountaintop experience — there seems to be no confusion, no euphoria, no recommitment or rededication to following God more faithfully. Samuel's heart does not, as Wesley's did, become "strangely warm." Instead, God delivers a harsh, even brutal message that Samuel must deliver to Eli, his mentor. It is a wonder that Samuel did not, like Jonah, try to run away from the nearly impossible task of telling a people they must change their ways.

Finally, be aware that Samuel needed the help of another person to recognize the call of God. Eli, who had not heard God's voice in a very long time, was the one who perceived that God was calling to Samuel. Sometimes, although God calls each of us at some time for some important mission or task, we need the help of the community to hear and understand God's call.

A retired school teacher in my class at seminary, told us how she ended up enrolling in a three-year M.Div. program, when she could have been thinking about cruises in the Caribbean. She had always been active in her church: directed the choir, led adult Bible study (Lay people can and should do this!), called on shut-ins during her summer vacations, served on all the boards and committees and was moderator a number of times. She had toyed with the idea of seminary way back before she started teaching. She universally got the message that she would make a great pastor's wife or, if she remained unmarried, a fine Christian educator. Not one single person encouraged her to pursue her dream; women, after all, did not belong in the pulpit telling men what to do. That is, until she was about to retire. Sitting around with other women of her church, knitting hats and mittens for the Christmas mitten tree, talking about what they were all going to do with the rest of their lives, the pastor's wife said (yes, the pastor's wife!), "Marjorie, why don't you go to seminary?" And Marjorie did. Again she heard the call, this time clearly, and she wasted no time. By the end of the summer, she had enrolled, sold her house and rented an apartment close to campus, bought some new clothes appropriate to student life rather than her teacher role. She graduated and went on to pastor a little church she was still serving when she died some ten years later. Sometimes we do not hear God's voice clearly enough, or we let the clamor of other voices drown out that "still, small voice." Sometimes we need God's voice mediated by another person or persons in words we positively understand. So it was with Samuel. And Marjorie, too.

Questions for Reflection and Discussion

- Have you ever experienced what you would define as a call from God? What were the circumstances? How did you respond? What did you ultimately decide to do? What factors helped you make the decision?

- Eli's sons have been blaspheming God. Eli has done his best to rebuke them, set them straight. They ignored him. If you are a parent, how as a person of faith, do you deal with children who disobey? display their contempt for your kind of religion? engage in behavior that you know will get them into trouble? How do you decide what to do and how to respond?

- Have you ever felt that God convicted you of some sin or failure? How did you react and what did you do?

- Have you ever felt that God called upon you to deliver a message of condemnation, as Samuel had to do? If you felt God needed you to speak up, were you able to do so? What made you decide one way or the other?

- The General Synod of the United Church of Christ voted that the entire church should work to become multi-racial, multi-cultural, open and affirming, and fully accessible. These are prophetic words grounded in scripture. Many local congregations have rejected that call, particularly as it relates to making their communities open to, and affirming of, people who are gay, lesbian, bisexual, or transgendered. How is your congregation responding to the call? How did it decide what stance to take? If you believe all God's children are welcome in the church, have you publicly said so? How did you arrive at the decision to speak or not speak?

• How do you pray?

• Samuel says, "Speak. I am listening." Do you set aside time to listen to what God has to say to you? How could you arrange for "listening time" in such a way that you could be faithful to it over a period of time?

• Write yourself a letter from God. Begin: Dear_____ and sign it, "God." Share your letter with a small group of two or three others. Do the words from God ring true? Does God say anything that you find surprising?

Closing

To the leader: Invite all participants to gather in a circle and hold hands. Ask each person to say a one sentence prayer about something learned or experienced or thought during the study time. Emphasize the prayer is to be one sentence. Ask if anyone would like to begin and then go around the circle to the right. When all have prayed, you may wish to say a few words of closing prayer.

Mark 14:3–9

SHE HAS DONE WHAT SHE COULD

Notes to the leader:

Although the text may seem very short, there is much here to be gleaned. Have participants read the story aloud in several different translations or have everyone read silently and then ask for people to volunteer to act out the story using their own words. Creating a little drama can make the story come powerfully alive.

If your focus center — candle and other objects has remained the same — change some things. Perhaps you could add another candle, use a different kind of flowers. You could also ask if anyone in the group would like to be responsible for the focus center or rotate the responsibility from week to week.

No matter where you meet for your study, but especially if you are meeting in homes, be sure that everyone can see and hear everyone else. Living rooms or family rooms often do not lend themselves to facilitating group interaction. Make sure no one is looking into someone else's back.

In Mark's gospel, the followers do not seem to grasp that Jesus' ministry is leading inevitably to Jerusalem and the cross. Time after time, they seem unaware that Jesus will so antagonize the authorities that his death is unavoidable.

However, the inescapable play of events is not lost on one unnamed woman. While Jesus was in the town of Bethany sharing a meal at the table of Simon the leper, the woman comes forward with an alabaster jar of nard, expensive perfume imported from India. She breaks the seal of the jar and pours the ointment over Jesus' head, an act which scandalizes some of the people who also are at table. Indignantly, they chastise the woman claiming that the perfume could have been sold for three hundred denarii, and the proceeds given to the poor. As one denarius was the usual day's wage for a common laborer, the ointment was worth a considerable sum.

Jesus rebukes the others, telling them to leave the woman alone. Not only does he accuse them, but he says that she has indeed "performed a good service" for him. He reminds them that poverty is unlikely to disappear, the poor being always in need of the benevolence of the righteous. But he will be with them only a short time longer, a fact that they have not yet understood.

Jesus then says, "She has done what she could; she has anointed my body beforehand for its burial." The woman, peripheral to Jesus' inner circle and probably not privy to his regular teaching, knows that his death will come too soon. What could she do? She could do what women were supposed to do — prepare the body of those who have died. Only in this case, the body is not yet dead, and costly ointments were reserved for persons of great power and authority. But she did not have all that many options. Women could not go out and about with Jesus; Jewish men did not talk to women out in public. But inside a house, conversation and/or contact were not forbidden. And so, the woman breaks open the jar and pours the perfume over Jesus' head, just as she would have, had he been already dead.

Jesus tells those who piously rebuke her, that the woman's deed will be remembered wherever the gospel is proclaimed in all the world. Her name will not go down in history, but her willingness to spare no expense to honor the one who gives her eternal life will remind generations of the need to do what we can for Christ in the world.

"She has done what she could." How often do we see few if any options? We are stuck, caught in the inevitable course of events, restricted by rules or conventions or our own lack of imagination to limited response in the face of tragedy or disaster or overwhelming calamity, or even ordinary, everyday loss. One of my professors in seminary told the story of the death of his own father. The old man had been failing for months, and the seminary community knew that it was but a matter of time before he died. Phil talked regularly about his father, remembering incidents, good times and bad; he felt that he was ready to lose his parent because he had been grieving and preparing himself for the final day. The old man died, and Phil was devastated in a way he never expected. And, of course, no one knew quite what to do to help or make things better.

One woman went to Phil's office, expressed her sympathy and said, "I've come simply to sit with you for awhile. I know I can't do anything to relieve your grief, but I'd just like to be with you." And so she sat down and was quiet. They did not talk. Phil did a few things at his desk and the woman read a bit, but mostly sat. After about an hour, she got up, hugged Phil, told him if he needed anything, to call. Then she left.

Phil told us about the woman and her gift. There really was nothing anyone could do to make things better. But the woman had done what she could — offered her presence and shared a small time of Phil's grief — respecting his need for quiet and honoring his need not to be alone.

Questions for Reflection and Discussion

- What do you imagine compelled the woman to perform such a lavish act? Have you ever given an extravagant gift? What were the circumstances? What made you decide to throw caution to the wind?

- The disciples react to the woman's gift with anger and criticism. What prompted them to respond in this way?

- Have you ever been the recipient of a gift you felt you did not deserve, or a gift you know cost the giver more than he or she could easily afford? How did you respond? What in your own personal history caused you to respond as you did?

- In this story, do you identify with the woman or with the disciples? What is your rationale?

- What does Jesus mean when he states that the poor will always be with us?

- Would the selling of the nard and the giving of the proceeds to the poor have made a difference?

- How does Jesus' statement about the poor influence your decisions about charity? about extravagant spending on yourself or others? about the problem of poverty in your neighborhood, your town, the world?

- Think of a time when you have felt the need to do something, but your responses have been limited by circumstances, or money, or other people's expectations. What did you decide to do? How did you reach your conclusion?

- When were you last extravagant in the name of faith? What prompted you?

Closing

Once again, gather your participants into a circle. Have ready a small squeeze bottle of baby oil and a supply of paper towels. Say, "The unnamed woman anointed Jesus with a very costly perfume. We are going to anoint each other with oil. I will start by pouring a little bit of oil into my own hand. Then I will anoint the hands of the person on my left, rubbing the oil into her/his hands. Then she/he will do the same to the next person and so on around the group." When you are finished with this activity, ask folks to be in prayer. Anyone who wishes to say a sentence prayer out loud may do so. Close with a very short prayer of your own, mentioning the lavishness of love.

Mark 1:16–20

FOLLOW ME...RIGHT NOW!

Notes to the leader:

You might want to start this session with a little game of Follow the Leader. Do silly things that will eventually make people reconsider and stop following you. When that happens, invite someone who has dropped out to be the leader. Play for a few more minutes: everyone should be laughing by the end. Discuss how it feels to be expected to do whatever the leader says or does. What made people drop out. What made some refuse to participate in the first place.

Act out this little scenario. You will need folks to be Simon, Peter, and Andrew, James and John, Zebedee, the hired hands, and Jesus. Encourage each person to really get into the part she/he is playing. Although there are few indications of the reactions of those left behind, your actors ought to be able to improvise.

Again, arrange the room so that everyone can see everyone else.

Jesus was recently baptized by John the Baptist; then he spent forty days in the wilderness, tempted by Satan, living with wild beasts, and cared for by angels. John gets arrested, and Jesus comes to Galilee. As he walks along the Sea of Galilee, he notices two fishers, brothers named Simon and Andrew, casting their nets into the water. Jesus calls to them, "Follow me and I will make you fish for people."

Oddly, they drop their nets immediately and go with Jesus. Jesus walks a little further and sees two more brothers, James and John, sons of Zebedee, who were in their boat mending nets. Jesus calls to both of them; they, too, immediately drop what they are doing. Leaving their father with the hired men, they follow Jesus.

What is going on here? Peter and Andrew, James and John leave their jobs and their families to follow Jesus, flaunting traditional responsibilities, to follow Jesus, whom they do not know. Oh, Jesus tells them they will be fishing for people, but that statement is hardly bait enough to cause them to abandon hearth and home and livelihood. The four men were undoubtedly necessary to their families' businesses, and their departure would cause a distinct hardship to those who remained at home. Also, although tradition would have us believe that the disciples were men of few means, these four were prosperous enough to have boats and houses and hired workers. Therefore, because of their immediate response to Jesus, we must conclude that the call they hear is a true call from God, a call to speak the good news, sharing Jesus' mission of preaching, teaching, healing, and driving out bad spirits.

Although I heard the call to ministry most clearly when I was twenty-five years old, I did not enter seminary until I was twenty-nine. How much easier life would have been had I dropped my nets and followed right away. For four years, the "hound of heaven" pursued me relentlessly as I tried my utmost to pretend God was not intruding into my comfortable life. What could God want with me? I didn't even like the church! If there was a safe place for hypocrites to hide, the church was surely it. The more I resisted, the more God rattled my cage. Finally, I acquiesced: I applied to one seminary and told myself that if admitted, I would go for a trial year. I was accepted and received thousands of dollars in scholarship and grant money without even asking.

Friends and family thought I was making, at best, a very peculiar decision. After all, I already had tenure in my teaching job, a job I really liked. Why would I unsettle a very satisfactory life by following God off into the wilderness? I can answer that question in only one way — God was not to be denied, no matter how reluctant I was.

And now I realize God was right. I love ministry and would not change this cutting-edge calling for all the tenure and tea in China. Just a note: I could have retired with thirty years in teaching December, 1999.

Questions for Reflection and Discussion

Notes to the leader:

Be sure to use a variety of groupings for discussion of the following questions: diads, triads, quads, etc. Change the configuration of the groups regularly so that people get to know all the members of your study class.

- What is your take on this story? How realistic is it that the four men literally dropped their nets and followed Jesus?

- This story brings to mind stories of people, both young and old, who leave family and friends and employment to join a cult or other "religious" group. Compare and contrast what happens in cults and what Jesus has in mind for the disciples.

- Have you ever made, or do you make, snap decisions? On paper, describe your decision making process. What steps do you take? Who do you consult? How long would a life-changing decision, like the one the four men made, take you?

- The story of Jesus calling the first four disciples makes very clear that God's call has implications far beyond the individual called. How would you respond if your spouse or partner came home with the news that she/he was quitting employment to preach the gospel full-time? How would you react to a young adult — son, daughter, grandson/daughter, niece or nephew?

• Most of us do not have the luxury of hearing God's call as clearly as did Peter and Andrew, James and John. For most of us call is much more subtle. Have you heard God's call? How did it come to you? How have you responded? What implications have there been for your loved ones?

• The United Church of Christ Statement of Faith contains the phrase, "the cost and joy of discipleship." What does it mean to be a disciple? What are the costs for you? the joys?

Closing

Notes to the leader:

Once again, gather your group into a circle holding hands. Invite each person to say a one-sentence prayer for the person on her/his right, praying in some way about discipleship and following Jesus. You should begin, and when all have prayed, close with a general prayer about discipleship.

Micah 6:(1–7), 8, (9–16)

WHAT DOES THE LORD REQUIRE?

◈

Notes to the leader:

As with Session One: The Sixth Day, this study needs the selected text put into context. Therefore, we will be looking at Micah 6:1–16 inclusive. Although verse 8 is very clear concerning what God expects of God's people, your Bible study group will be significantly helped to understand why God felt the need to communicate in so firm and unequivocal a manner, if they understand the transgressions of the leadership and people of Israel.

The entire book of Micah, although very brief, presents our God acting in what sometimes seem to be contradictory ways. God is creative, calling the worlds into being, making humanity in the divine image. God is compassionate and loving, forgiving and uplifting, transforming and merciful. God is also very angry at times, capable of destroying creation and the chosen people Israel. But God's distressing behavior is never capricious; it comes in response to sin, to the people forgetting who and whose they are and what responsibilities are required of them.

<u>Verses 1-2</u> The setting is the courtroom. Israel has broken the covenant, and God invites Israel to plead its case before the mountains and the hills, which have been around since the beginning of time. They were present when the covenant was made, and they were there to see the promises broken. God is fed up and is punishing the people.

Verses 3-5 God reiterates all that God has done for the people: brought them out of slavery in Egypt, gave them wonderful leaders — Moses, Aaron, and Miriam, brought them into the promised land across the Jordan River. If the people will only remember this and other saving acts, they will not wander from God's way.

Verses 6-7 God has done wonderful and mighty deeds for Israel, and God expects something in return. The prophet asks the questions about what will be pleasing to God — bowing, burnt offerings, a calf a year old; how about thousands of rams and rivers of oil; even a first born child? It seems that none of these traditional offerings is what God requires. God wants something far more diffi- cult to give than possessions (Children, like wives, were the possession of husbands and fathers). The questions push to the extreme. Is there nothing that Israel can give that will be pleasing to God?

Verse 8 God's answer to the question, "What can we do to please God," changes the question. The people are look- ing for some religious ceremony or ritual that will get them off the hook. They are preoccupied with superficial acts of piety, rather than substantive changes in behavior. Micah tells them clearly that God is much more interested in how they live their daily lives than in what they do when they gather for worship.

Micah tells the people what God expects in a threefold answer to their question: do justice, love kindness, walk humbly with God. Sounds easy enough, but the words are packed; they mean more than might be ascertained at first glance. "Justice" is an action, an activity people do. It is not enough to long for justice or praise it if it happens or whine about it if it is wanting. God is calling on the peo- ple to work for justice, to incorporate fairness in their daily activity, to struggle for equality for all people — especially those who cannot engage in the conflict on their own behalf. "Kindness" is much more than simple sweetness and a good deed or two. In this context, kindness conveys loyalty, fidelity, love — whether in relationships with other people or in covenant with God. God is not looking for a covenant people who obey out of fear of reprisal; God wants Israel's faithfulness to be born of love.

Finally, Israel is to walk humbly with God. God is to be first in the lives of the people, not something relegated to special worship times or convenience. The walk with God is to be a life-long activity of putting God first and conforming to God's will.

God's answer to the question, "What can we do to please you," demands a lifestyle change, an examination of ethics and values. Israel and we are to abandon the notion that God will be satisfied with ceremony and ritual on holy days. God demands our entire lives, lived in covenant, and nothing less.

Verses 9-12 Again God reminds the people what is intolerable — the lying, the cheating, the stealing — all in the name of business. God cannot be God and not respond in anger with punishment to the dishonesty and injustice that has become commonplace in Israel. Punishment for such despicable behavior is just and justified. God has reminded the people of all that God has done on their behalf, and all that they have done in response. It is no wonder that God seeks to punish them.

Verses 13-16 And punish them God does, in justice and righteousness, because of their sins. God inflicts upon Israel a series of what are sometimes called futility curses. They will eat but not be satisfied; put away but never save; sow but not reap, tread olives but do no anointing, stomp grapes but drink no wine. God accuses the people of following Omri and his son, Ahab, obeying their statutes rather than conforming to the covenant with God. Not only will Israel suffer the curses, but God will give them over to ruin and ridicule, make them objects of scorn and derision. They will be the laughingstock of other nations.

Do justice, love kindness, walk humbly with God. Think about those eight little words. What sort of implication do they have for our lives? I was teaching an adult class called *Christian Care Giving: A Way of Life*. We had met for two months, once a week to struggle with what it means to use our specifically Christian gifts — prayer, scripture, blessing, etc. — to help other people. During our final meeting, Mabel suggested that we start a hunger program to help feed the homeless and working poor, so prominently evident, but so easily ignored in downtown Akron, Ohio. We were a downtown church which had taken little responsibility for the residents of our neighborhood, which was just fine with a large contingency of the congregation. With the help of the Holy Spirit and about a dozen other folks, Mabel got the program going.

Once a month, we prepared a huge meal, more like Thanksgiving dinner than Saturday lunch, entertained our guests with live piano music, and gave them clothing, health and hygiene products, and our friendship. Everyone who wanted it also got a brown bag meal for later in the day. Mabel cooked and supervised in the kitchen as if it were her own home and our guests were to the finest folk society had to offer. She welcomed folks and made them feel at home. She talked with young mothers with children, old men who needed a bath and a shave, the homeless folk who were often struggling with mental illnesses, too little supervision, and too much access to alcohol. Mabel opened her arms to all of them. Some Saturdays more than 225 persons sat down and broke bread with us, because Mabel sought to do justice and love kindness. Twelve years later the program goes on, funded by grants and staffed by volunteers led by Mabel, who never wants to take too much credit for all that she and her idea have done for hundreds, maybe thousands, of friends in downtown Akron. I think Mabel walks humbly with her God, as well.

Questions for Reflection and Discussion

- The church has generally skimmed over the texts in the Bible that deal with God's anger. We do not like to deal with them because they are deeply troubling. Has your pastor preached about God's anger in your recent memory? Do you think you have ever experienced the anger of God? What were the circumstances? How does the possibility of God's anger influence your decision making and behavior?

- What does God want from us in the church? from you? Can we ever be good enough?

- Think of your Sunday morning worship. Do you think God is pleased by what happens in your church on Sunday morning? What's right and what's wrong about it? What would you change if you could?

- God does not want occasional acts of piety; God clearly desires that our whole lives be lived doing justice, loving kindness, and walking humbly with God. All of a sudden that easy, threefold sentence takes on enormous proportions. How are you living out God's command? What is justice? kindness? walking humbly with God? What do these three injunctions have to do with "real life"?

- God is going to punish Israel for living debauched lives, for lying, cheating and stealing. Have you ever felt that God was punishing you? Was God just? Is punishment ever just? Does it accomplish what it is supposed to accomplish?

- Imagine you are Micah. What is your response to God's plan that you tell the people of Israel they have sinned and will be punished? In your own life, when have you had to act as a prophet? Were you a willing prophet, or like some biblical prophets who tried to run away from the responsibility God gave them?

- What does it mean to walk humbly with God? Some scholars suggest the word should not be "humbly," but rather "carefully." How is the meaning of the walk with God changed?

- The United Church of Christ is seeking to become multi-racial, multi-cultural, open and affirming, and accessible to all in all its local congregations. How does this mandate aspire to address God's requirements? What are your feelings about the mandate? Have you or will you push your congregation to truly open its doors to all God's children? What can you do?

Closing

Note to the leader:

Gather your group into a circle and request them to hold hands. Each person is invited to offer a one sentence prayer for him/herself. Praying for oneself in public is very difficult for some folks. However, by now you should have developed a significant level of trust within your group. Ask for a volunteer to go first. Reassure everyone that it is all right to pass or not participate. When all who wish have prayed, close with a general prayer for help in doing what God requires.

Matthew 22:34–40

THE GREAT COMMANDMENT

Notes for the leader:

To the leader: As Matthew 22:34–40 is the last lesson in this series, you may want to plan for participants to evaluate the entire series and what they have learned before you adjourn for the final time. Written evaluations get the most honest responses, while oral evaluations, especially if you write responses on newsprint, help shy folks think of what to say. If you use written evaluations, prepare a form ahead of time; if you plan to evaluate orally, prepare the questions ahead of time. Include some questions that require reflection on making decisions based on scripture and faith.

Matthew 22:34–40 is a short, easy little passage that you might want to have read aloud from a number of different translations. It also could be acted out concentrating on the initial couple of sentences where the Pharisees are plotting for some way to trick Jesus, and on the Pharisees' response to what Jesus tells them. You will need a group to be the Pharisees and someone to be Jesus.

The Gospel of Matthew should be read as a sacred text of an ongoing religion — Judaism. The writer saw his work and the community for which he wrote as a continuation of

Judaism, not as the beginning of a new religion — Christianity.

He did, however, interpret those leaders who rejected Jesus — the Pharisees, high priests, and Sadducees — as giving up their claim to be the people of God.

Matthew speaks of love and right relationship and the importance of the law in Jesus' Sermon on the Mount. You may want to review Matthew 5:17–48 just to set The Great Commandment in a context of teachings. By reading both texts, you will more clearly see that Jesus had no intention of wiping away all the law that had come before. As a matter of fact, Jesus reinforces the importance of the law and expands upon it, finally fulfilling it in Matthew 22:34–40.

As they have been for a number of chapters, the religious leaders are very distressed with Jesus, his teachings, and his popularity. They look for ways to entrap him and discredit him. What better way to undermine the teaching of an itinerant preacher, than by employing the skills of a lawyer to entrap this uneducated upstart, who poses such a threat to their authority. Rabbinical teachers did not consider one commandment to be more important than any other commandment. All commandments were of equal value and importance. Ranking them would simply be the postulation of people looking for a way to organize or prioritize. So, as all divine law was equally binding, the lawyer was perhaps trying to fool Jesus into declaring one part more significant than another.

But Jesus is not to be outwitted. Jesus' first part of The Great Commandment is a restatement of the first part of the Shema (Deuteronomy 6:4–9): "You shall love the Lord your God with all your heart, and with all your soul, and with all your might." This reiteration clearly is nothing new. Then Jesus adds to the centuries old injunction that there is a second commandment like it, "You shall love your neighbor as yourself."

Notice that the "second like it" commandment is given no less importance. The second is equal to the first, does not supplant the first, but is to be lived out at the same time as the first. Jesus goes on to say that "on these two commandments hang all the law and the prophets." Jesus' bold and challenging statement is not just a summary of all the laws that have directed Israel's life. Nor is it a sort of beginning rubric from which all other laws and prophetic utterances can be derived. Instead, Jesus' great commandment is the yardstick against which all laws and prophecies are to be judged.

What a radical and unsettling declaration! Although the text does not so state, the religious leaders must have reeled. They could easily subscribe to the directive to love God. But love neighbor as self? What did that mean? Who was the neighbor? What does it mean to love self? The law and prophets may have sufficed for many lifetimes, but now Jesus was telling the religious leaders that everything that grounded their lives in right relationship with God and other people must be measured against the great commandment. How Earth must have shuddered. How the ground must have heaved. How the sky must have swirled and gone sunless and blank. On what could they depend anymore?

Their daughter was an honor student, a creative writing major whose future was open and rife with possibilities. Before she even finished her junior year, she had been offered several career opportunities in large advertising agencies. Her parents were proud of her, and excited about her potential to make a large salary, and live a very comfortable life.

But midway through her senior year, the daughter announced to her stunned parents that she was signing up for a program that placed talented graduates in failing schools, both inner city and rural, to teach children who may or may not have any interest in their own education. Her parents objected, pleaded, threatened — all to no avail.

Why, they asked, was she throwing away her talents on a bunch of ungrateful kids in a dangerous neighborhood, where her life might be in jeopardy?

She responded that all those years they had made her go to Sunday School and church had rubbed off. She felt called by God to use her gifts in the service of others, especially children. She'd spent hours and days and months praying and talking with God about how she could best demonstrate her sincere love of God and human beings.

Ten years later, she is still working in a rural school in Appalachia, teaching children and helping them discover their own gifts of creative writing. She could not be happier.

Questions for Reflection and Discussion

Notes for the leader:

Small groups may best facilitate some of the questions. But as this is your final time with the participants, whole group discussion is equally important.

- What is love? Are there different kinds of love? What might they be?

- Look at Matthew 5:17–48. Notice especially the statements that begin, "You have heard that it was said. . . ." These are some of Jesus' most difficult teachings. If this is love, can you do it? If these statements are the yardstick against which we measure our behavior, how are we doing?

- What does it mean to love God with all that we are? How does this charge influence your decision making? How does it challenge your distribution of monies?

- What does it mean to love your neighbor as yourself? Who is your neighbor? How does this directive challenge your decision making?

- On a scale of one to ten, ten being the highest, what kind of lover are you?

- Do you think the great commandment applies equally to corporate life as well as individual? Justify your answer with a story from your own experience.

- In what ways do you need to grow in love? toward God? toward your family? toward your friends? toward your enemies? toward those you do not know?

Closing

To the leader: Do your evaluation before you assemble the group for its final moments together. Ask your participants to once again gather in a circle and hold hands. Invite people to share, as they are able, one or two things that they will take home with them from these six weeks you have spent together. Close with a time of prayer in which each person will pray a two sentence prayer. Sentence one will mention something the person is thankful for that happened in the context of this Bible study. The second sentence will be a petition for help in some area of the person's life, where she or he needs to grow in order to better live out the great commandment. When all have prayed, close with a prayer that lifts up the gifts you have shared and been given in this study time, for the illumination of God's word through group study, for the gifts of each other and the friendship that has been deepened.

My guess is that people will ask you when the next study begins.

Other books from The Pilgrim Press:

Bad Girls of the Bible

Exploring women of Questionable Virtue

Barbara J. Essex

0-8298-1339-X/144 pages/paper/$13.95

Designed as a 14 week study, Bad Girls explores the Bible's accounts of traditionally misunderstood or despised women. Essex offers fresh new interpretations of women such as Delilah, Jezebel, and Sapphira. She includes biblical exegesis understandable to lay persons.

Moon Under Her Feet

Women of the Apocalyse

Kim S. Vidal

0-8298-1415-9/128 pages/paper/$10.00

Moon Under Her Feet is a guide to discover and understand the symbolic meanings of the female images in the Book of Revelation. It includes eleven sessions. Eash session includes background information and scriptural references as well as discussion questions, songs, prayers, and responsive readings.

To order call, 1-800-537-3394; Fax 216-736-2206
Or visit our web site at www.pilgrimpress.com. Prices do not include shipping and handling. Prices are subject to change without notice.

Other books from the Insights Series includes:

9 781608 992249